D1511583

COLLECTIVE
Biographies

Great Magicians
and Illusionists

John Allen

ReferencePoint
Press®

San Diego, CA

© 2017 ReferencePoint Press, Inc.
Printed in the United States

For more information, contact:
ReferencePoint Press, Inc.
PO Box 27779
San Diego, CA 92198
www.ReferencePointPress.com

LIBRARY OF CONGRESS CATALOGING-IN-PUBLICATION DATA

Names: Allen, John, 1957-
Title: Great magicians and illusionists / by John Allen.
Description: San Diego, CA : ReferencePoint Press, Inc., 2017. | Series:
   Collective biographies series | Includes bibliographical references and index.
Identifiers: LCCN 2016020681 (print) | LCCN 2016020907 (ebook) | ISBN
   9781601529985 (hardback) | ISBN 9781601529992 (eBook)
Subjects: LCSH: Magicians--Biography--Juvenile literature.
Classification: LCC GV1545.A2 A44 2017 (print) | LCC GV1545.A2 (ebook) | DDC
   793.8092 [B] --dc23
LC record available at https://lccn.loc.gov/2016020681

CONTENTS

INTRODUCTION   The Pleasure of Being Fooled

Magicians depend on the fact that audiences like to be deceived. The history of stage magic is one long proof of this. Conjuring, as magic once was called, is among the oldest forms of entertainment. For centuries street performers have fooled people with sleight of hand using cups and balls, coins, cards, and other small objects. In the 1840s the French magician Jean Eugene Robert-Houdin raised the magic show from streets and circuses to elegant drawing rooms and the popular stage. Dubbed "the father of modern magic," Robert-Houdin employed mind-reading tricks and devised amazing illusions, such as catching bullets shot from a gun and making an orange tree grow fruit before the audience's eyes. Magicians adopted the great Robert-Houdin's sophisticated patter—his witty way of talking to the audience—and his habit of wearing formal evening attire onstage. The magic act became a staple of the British music hall and the vaudeville circuit in America. Magicians competed furiously to come up with ever more astonishing illusions, and the best performers became linked to their most popular tricks. Among these were the Liverpool-born Colonel Stodare's Sphinx illusion of the 1860s, in which the living head of an Egyptian appeared in a box on a tabletop; American

Harry Kellar's Princess Karnac trick of the early 1900s, in which a woman levitates in the air; and Harry Blackstone Sr.'s Floating Light Bulb of the 1930s, in which a lighted bulb was taken from a lamp and made to float, still glowing, through hoops and above the heads of the audience. Today's magicians have their own specialties, such as David Blaine's Frozen in Time illusion, which saw the magician encased in a block of ice in Times Square for sixty-three hours.

Making Use of Technology

Through the years professional magicians have had to adjust their routines for different media and venues, from live performance to film and from TV to close scrutiny on the Internet and social media. Sometimes modern technology—such as the dazzling digital effects in movies—can make stage magic seem quaint and outdated. Yet the best of today's performers make use of science in their acts just as magicians have always done. As long as people believe that a trick is not just pure technology, that it is based somehow on the magician's skill and cleverness, they will happily submit to being fooled. "We've got this really rich history of magic and technology going together," says British illusionist Kieron Kirkland. "The whole point behind doing a magic trick is you're trying to shape and control people's behavior. And, at the heart of technology, that's what it's about as well."[1]

But technology is only part of the story. Alex Stone, author of the book *Fooling Houdini*, thinks magic's enduring popularity has to do with basic human nature. "To truly understand the art of magic and its timeless appeal, you wind up asking questions not just about how the mind works—and why sometimes it doesn't—but also about some of the most fundamental aspects

> "To truly understand the art of magic and its timeless appeal, you wind up asking questions not just about how the mind works . . . but also about some of the most fundamental aspects of human nature."[2]
>
> —Alex Stone, author of the book Fooling Houdini

A magician uses sleight of hand to perform a card trick. Although magicians and illusionists have developed many sophisticated techniques over the years, they have always depended on the fact that audiences like to be deceived.

of human nature," says Stone. "Why do people take pleasure in deceiving others? How does the brain perceive the world and parse everyday experience?. . . What is reality, and how much of it do we consciously take in?"[2]

Breaking the Code of Silence

To keep their audiences mystified, magicians and illusionists have always been fiercely protective of their trade secrets. But modern technology has affected this part of the business as well. The torrent of information available online ensures that the secret of how a trick is done is often just a click away. The magicians' traditional code of silence about such things no longer holds. In 1998 veteran magicians were horrified when the FOX network broadcast a series of prime-time specials that revealed the secrets behind some of the most celebrated illusions in history. The shows got huge ratings, leading some to predict disaster for the magicians' trade. Instead, crowds for magic shows in Las Vegas and elsewhere continued as large as ever. With a few tweaks here and there, the old tricks still could leave audiences astounded. Jim Steinmeyer, who has worked behind the scenes to devise some of modern magic's greatest illusions, maintains that the key is not the trick itself but the artistry of the magician. "The success of a magician lies in making a human connection to the magic, the precise focus that creates a fully realized illusion in the minds of the audience," says Steinmeyer. "The simple explanation is that seldom do the crude gimmicks in a magic show—those mirrors, threads, or rubber bands—deceive people. The audience is taken by the hand and led to deceive themselves."[3] For in the end they enjoy being fooled.

> "The success of a magician lies in making a human connection to the magic. . . . The audience is taken by the hand and led to deceive themselves."[3]
>
> —Jim Steinmeyer, author of a book on the history of magic effects

CHAPTER 1

Harry Houdini

On September 21, 1912, the audience inside the Circus Busch in Berlin, Germany, leans forward in anticipation. The famous American magician Harry Houdini instructs his assistants to lock his feet into stocks. Next to Houdini is a large tank of mahogany and steel filled with water. The tank features a steel grill inside and a front plate of transparent glass. Houdini is hoisted by ropes until he is hovering upside down over the tank. He takes several deep breaths and nods to his assistants. In full view of the German crowd, he is lowered into the tank, water splashing over the sides as he goes. The stocks are then locked into place atop the cell, securing his feet. With a flourish Houdini's assistants draw curtains all around the tank. The orchestra plays as the audience holds its breath. One rubber-coated assistant stands off to the side clutching an ax in case he has to smash the glass and rescue the magician. Forty seconds go by, seemingly an eternity. At last there is a slight flutter of the curtain. Then it is ripped aside to reveal Houdini, dripping wet, eyes bloodshot, specks of foam on his lip, standing upright in triumph. The crowd leaps to its feet, shaking the walls of the theater with thunderous cheers and applause. The Water Torture Cell—or Upside Down, as Houdini dubbed the trick—has to be one of the most thrilling magic effects in history. Certainly it leaves no doubt in the public's mind that Harry Houdini is the greatest escape artist in the world. As Houdini would often claim, "No prison can hold me; no hand or leg irons or steel locks can shackle me. No ropes or chains can keep me from my freedom."[4]

Fascination with Locks

Harry Houdini was born Ehrich Weisz on March 24, 1874, in Budapest, Hungary. One of seven children, Ehrich was the son of Mayer Weisz (later changed to Weiss) and his wife Cecilia. Ehrich was two when his family sailed to the United States. They settled in Appleton, Wisconsin, where Mayer found a position as a rabbi. But soon his congregation rejected him as being too old and set in his ways. The family moved to Milwaukee, where they struggled to make ends meet. As a young boy Ehrich quit school to work like his brothers and sisters. He shined shoes and sold newspapers, and also spent time at a local hardware shop that sold all kinds of locks. Ehrich—called Ehry or Harry by his family—became fascinated with locks, practicing every spare moment at home to spring open closets and pantries with a small buttonhook.

> "No prison can hold me; no hand or leg irons or steel locks can shackle me. No ropes or chains can keep me from my freedom."[4]
>
> —Harry Houdini

He also was enthralled with an acrobat he saw at a street circus, an expert who could walk across a wire stretched twenty feet in the air between two poles. Soon, after hours of practice and a series of painful falls, he mastered the trick himself on a rope in his backyard. Ehrich decided that performing in public was the life for him.

From sheer boredom Ehrich ran away from home at age twelve, but soon returned. As a teenager he showed physical prowess by excelling in running, cycling, swimming, and boxing. He also discovered a book that would change his life:

The Memoirs of Robert-Houdin. The great French magician's autobiography convinced Ehrich to study the techniques of magic with an eye to a career as a performer. For his stage name he added an *i* to his hero's name, turning Houdin into Houdini. Working first with a friend and then with his brother as the Brothers Houdini, Harry played fairs and amusement parks in the early 1890s. At age twenty he met and married Wilhelmina Beatrice Rahner. Bess, as he called her, became his partner onstage as well, assisting him with mind-reading stunts, comedy routines, and magic tricks of every description. Houdini's tricks were mostly the standard ones of the time. For the Metamorphosis, he and Bess would change places in a trunk in a matter of seconds. In the Hindoo Needle Trick, Houdini would seem to swallow forty needles only to spit them out again—now linked in an unbroken chain.

> "[Houdini's escape from handcuffs] was such a marvelous performance that many in the audience were convinced that he was 'in league with the spirits.'"[5]
>
> —William Kalush and Larry Sloman, biographers of Houdini

A New Specialty

In addition to performing magic tricks, Houdini would use his expertise with locks to escape from handcuffs onstage. Then, around 1896, he hit on a brilliant, crowd-pleasing idea. He would announce to the audience he could easily free himself from the handcuffs and restraints used by the local police. Often he would enlist officers to come onstage and affirm that the handcuffs were genuine and properly locked onto his wrists. Houdini's biographers William Kalush and Larry Sloman describe one such demonstration in New Brunswick, New Jersey:

> Officer Baxter and private citizens Arthur McGinley and John McCafferty strode onstage laden with heavy chains, handcuffs, and leg irons. They wrapped the chains around his body and handcuffed Houdini with his hands behind

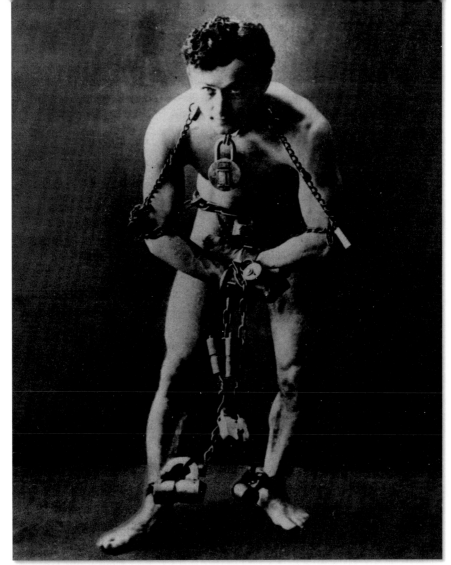

Harry Houdini, considered by many to be the world's greatest escape artist, is shown in chains sometime around 1899 during one of his many shows. Houdini's tricks always astounded his audiences.

his back. At the same time they shackled his feet. Helped into his small curtained cabinet that he called his "ghost box," he took only minutes to emerge a free man. It was such a marvelous performance that many in the audience were convinced that he was "in league with the spirits."[5]

Houdini's new specialty made him a star. His ability to escape from handcuffs and shackles captured the public's imagination

Houdini's Escape Secrets

As the master escape artist of his day, Houdini used physical skill, technical knowledge, and trickery in his act. To earn his reputation as the Handcuff King, he started with his lifelong knowledge of locks and locking devices. He collected locks and studied them closely. His photographic memory helped him recall how each one worked and could be opened. To open a pair of handcuffs on stage, he often concealed a key on his person or with an assistant. Even while cuffed, he could manipulate a key with his hands or with his teeth. Sometimes his process was much simpler. For example, certain handcuffs could be opened by banging them on a hard surface, such as a lead plate hidden under his trousers. He even resorted to fake handcuffs, which were made to fool nonexperts and could be easily opened by removal of a rivet. "Remember it is not the trick that is to be considered," he once said, "but the style and manner in which it is presented."

Houdini's straitjacket escape was a specialty that combined clever technique with brute strength. He would puff out his chest while being strapped into the jacket, giving him some breathing room. He would then jerk about violently and with great effort manage to pass his head under one elbow until he had worked his arms free in front of his body. In the process he would almost dislocate his shoulder. Then he would undo the buckles and straps with his teeth.

Quoted in PBS, "Houdini—Escape Secrets: Handcuff Escapes." www.pbs.org.

and earned him reams of free publicity from local newspapers. Sometimes he would set up outdoor performances to draw larger crowds. To add an extra dash of danger, he might plunge into a river while handcuffed. Soon he was performing escapes not only from handcuffs but from straitjackets, coffins, and jails. One of Houdini's most popular tricks was his brother Theo's idea. He would free himself from a straitjacket while standing at center stage in full view of the audience.

The *Mirror* Challenge

Houdini's stage act soon became a worldwide sensation. In 1904 the Handcuff King, as Houdini billed himself, crossed the ocean and broke attendance records at theaters throughout England, Scotland, and Wales. People flocked to see the cocky young Yank issue his customary challenge for handcuffs that could hold him. Ordinarily he would free himself from all the submitted handcuffs with ease. However, one evening at the Hippodrome Theatre in London's West End, a reporter from the *Daily Illustrated Mirror* handed the magician a pair of specially made steel handcuffs. The crowd murmured when Houdini examined the cuffs and refused three times to put them on. The *Mirror* handcuffs, the product of five years' work by a veteran Birmingham blacksmith, featured a lock that local experts believed could not be picked. Houdini saw at once that they would present an extraordinary challenge.

Five days later Houdini accepted the challenge at a special sold-out matinee performance. He seemed surprisingly humble. "I do not know whether I am going to get out or not," he told the audience. "But I can assure you I am going to try my best."[6] Once the handcuffs were snapped on, Houdini withdrew into a small cabinet. After twenty minutes he popped his head out to examine the lock in a brighter light. At thirty-five minutes he appeared again, his face pouring sweat, to stretch his cramping legs. Nearly an hour had gone by when he emerged and asked to have the cuffs removed for a moment so he could take off his coat. When the *Mirror* reporter refused unless Houdini admitted defeat, the magician managed to pull a penknife from his pocket, open it with his teeth, throw his coat over his head, and cut it off by the seams. Although he returned to the cabinet, which began to rock from his exertions, the crowd sensed he was beaten. Then suddenly Houdini sprang from the cabinet and held the shiny handcuffs aloft for everyone to see. It had taken an hour and ten minutes, but he was free. The crowd roared its approval. Some spectators lifted the spent magician on their shoulders and paraded him around the theater. Houdini wrote later, "I must say it was one of the hardest, but at the same time one of the fairest, tests I ever had."[7]

A Step Ahead of His Rivals

To build his legend Houdini worked hard to come up with daring new escapes. He was driven to stay one step ahead of his many rivals. "Once Houdini's exploits blazed across newspaper headlines, the opportunists, the cunning, the nutcases, and the jealous emerged like theatrical chameleons," writes Houdini's biographer Sid Fleischman. "The imitators not only parted their hair in the middle, as did the escape artist, they mimicked his style of dress and his billing. There were more self-crowned Kings of Handcuffs before the footlights than in all the royal houses of Europe—half a hundred in England alone."[8]

One of Houdini's most popular routines was the Milk Can Escape, a trick he called the best he ever invented. Its tagline on promotional posters was "Failure Means a Drowning Death."[9] Clad in a bathing suit, Houdini would be handcuffed and sealed inside a large milk can filled to the brim with pails of water. Once a curtain was drawn, Houdini would perform his escape and reappear, soaking wet but free, to the cheers of the crowd. The key to the trick was the lid of the can, which was nearly impossible to open from the outside but quite easy to push out from the inside. Maintaining his status required Houdini to devise new wrinkles for his older tricks. For example, in 1911, years after he had first performed the Milk Can Escape, he debuted the Water Torture Cell, a fiendishly clever upgrade. Houdini spent more than $10,000 to have the glass-faced cell of steel and mahogany specially built. He copyrighted the illusion as a one-act play, and it became a staple of his vaudeville act and road shows.

> "The imitators not only parted their hair in the middle, as did the escape artist, they mimicked his style of dress and his billing."[8]
>
> —Sid Fleischman, Houdini's biographer

Year after year Houdini dreamed up new modes of escape. He would wriggle free from a straitjacket while suspended upside down from a crane. He would be thrown into the ocean from a tugboat while in handcuffs and leg irons. He would escape from crates, trunks, and prison cells. Houdini seemed desperate to challenge himself again and again and obliterate all his rivals.

Attack on Robert-Houdin

Houdini's fierce desire to be the best in the world of magic often led him to belittle others' accomplishments. This even held true with

Houdini is about to step inside a packing crate that will be lowered into the ice-covered Detroit River in 1907. Time and again he managed to miraculously escape from straitjackets, handcuffs, and leg irons as well as from crates, trunks, and even prison cells.

his idol, Robert-Houdin. While gathering material for a proposed encyclopedia of magic, Houdini interviewed several old-time magicians who claimed to have known the deceased French master or witnessed his famous act. One told Houdini that Robert-Houdin had stolen many tricks invented by others, while a disgruntled German conjurer insisted that the Frenchman had not even written his famous *Memoirs*, instead hiring out the job. Houdini, an astute judge of human character, would ordinarily have seen through the scurrilous reports as mere jealousy on the part of these old performers. But Houdini himself—who only the year before had reverently placed flowers at Robert-Houdin's grave—seemed bent on knocking his French idol from his pedestal. Perhaps he thought it would make his own name shine forth all the brighter as the king of magic. In any case, instead of an encyclopedia on the history of magic, in 1908 he published *The Unmasking of Robert-Houdin*, a spiteful book that portrayed the French magician as hopelessly overrated, a thief and a fraud. When the book's lies and half-truths

Houdini and the Creator of Sherlock Holmes

Following the death of his mother in 1913, Houdini became interested in the spirit world and attempts to contact the dead. In the course of his investigations, he struck up a friendship with Arthur Conan Doyle, the British creator of the great detective Sherlock Holmes. The two had a great deal in common. Both operated by logic—Doyle having been a practicing physician before he began to write detective stories—and both were well versed in entertaining the public with misdirection and deceit. They shared a fascination with the idea of life after death, although they approached the subject very differently. Unlike Houdini, who sought solid proof that spirits existed, Doyle had long been a true believer. He even belonged to the British Society for Psychical Research, whose members included some of the top statesmen and scientists of the day.

In 1924 Doyle touted an attractive young medium named Mina Crandon, nicknamed Margery, as the real item. A panel from *Scientific American* attended more than twenty of Margery's séances and was taken in by the antics of "Walter," the spirit she summoned. It was Walter who supposedly spoke in the dark and caused the table to levitate and bells to ring. On his first visit to one of Margery's séances, Houdini saw through her tricks—how with her husband's help she lifted the table and manipulated the bell. When Houdini exposed Margery in a pamphlet, Doyle, still a believer, ended his friendship with the magician.

were challenged by reviewers, particularly angry French writers, Houdini lashed out in response. "In the Robert-Houdin articles [collected in the book] we fairly revolutionized the history of magic," Houdini claimed. "Robert-Houdin has been uncrowned as the king of conjuring and automata [stage machinery], and the crown has been distributed, bit by bit, among the earlier magicians to whom it rightfully belonged. Men on two continents who once proclaimed Robert-Houdin as magic's hero now refer to him as the Prince of Pilferers."[10] Ultimately Houdini's warped account backfired on him. Historians of magic consider his book a travesty, and Robert-Houdin's reputation remains secure.

Spiritualism and Untimely Death

Houdini's own career continued to flourish. His tours of European capitals drew huge crowds. In 1918 he astonished onlookers at the Hippodrome Theater in New York City with the best of his pure illusions—making a full-grown Asian elephant disappear from inside a large wooden box the size of a garage. Houdini's popularity also led him to start his own film company and make movies. He starred as the Master Detective, a character named Quentin Locke, who would perform incredible escapes while also saving women in peril and nabbing criminals. Houdini's acting drew mixed reviews, but audiences loved to see him struggle out of a straitjacket or escape from a padlocked cell, with no camera tricks needed.

In his later years Houdini developed an interest in spiritualism, the attempt to contact the spirits of the dead. At first he had hopes of communicating with his dead mother, but soon he turned to exposing phony mediums—those who claimed the ability to contact the dead and would take advantage of gullible clients. Houdini's expert knowledge of magic and his longtime habit of pointing out the scams of his competitors served him well in his mission. Where even scientists and scholars were often fooled, it was easy for him to spot the hidden devices and wires used to produce ghostly effects in séances.

In 1926, riding high as ever in the entertainment world, Houdini endured what seemed at first a minor setback. To demonstrate his amazing body control, he sometimes would tighten his stomach muscles and submit to a punch in the abdomen. One night in Detroit, while suffering from a mild fever and a broken ankle, Houdini allowed a college student to hit him several times in his midsection. Despite unusual discomfort from the blows, he went on with the evening's performance. The next day a doctor examined Houdini, diagnosing acute appendicitis and recommending immediate surgery. Houdini at first refused, but later was rushed to the hospital for removal of a ruptured appendix. However, peritonitis—infection of the abdomen's inner wall—had set in and was too far advanced. Houdini died on Halloween, October 31, 1926, at age fifty-two. Although he thought spiritualism a fraud, before he died the great magician promised his wife Bess to contact her from the other side if possible. A séance she organized ten years later produced only silence.

CHAPTER 2

Penn & Teller

On the sleek stage at the Rio Hotel in Las Vegas, Nevada, Penn & Teller are in their element. Penn Jillette, six foot six with a ponytail and clad in vest and tie like a hip stockbroker, announces what he calls a stupid escape trick and hustles up into the audience to pick a volunteer. As usual, Teller, red-haired and tiny in a sober vest, stands to the side without a word. Penn then explains that Teller will escape from an enormous trash bag filled with helium from a tank onstage. While Penn remarks that helium is a deadly gas but a fun one for filling up balloons, Teller steps into the black plastic bag. The volunteer cinches the straps at the top while Penn slips a tube inside and inflates the bag with helium. "You OK in there, Teller?"[11] Penn calls out. Teller says he's OK, in a high-pitched helium-filled voice that gets a huge laugh. Then the stage goes dark and Penn flashes a digital camera. When the lights come back a second later, Teller is standing beside Penn, looking at the picture on the camera, while the volunteer holds the helium-filled bag floating over his head. Stunned at the instantaneous switch, the audience applauds with delight. With a simple trash bag and a tank of helium, Penn & Teller have revived an old escape trick and added a few laughs into the bargain.

Magic as a Comic Deception

Penn & Teller, considered by many to be the greatest comedy magic act in history, seem oddly matched as performers. Penn is tall, brash, and opinionated, while Teller is short, quiet, and reflective. Yet they have managed to work together with spectacular success for more than forty years. Raymond Joseph Teller was born in Philadelphia, Pennsylvania, on February 14, 1948, of Russian, Jewish, and Cuban descent. Penn Jillette, his younger associate, was born in Greenfield, Massachusetts, on March 5, 1955. Both became interested in magic at a young age. Teller was five years old when, laid up at home with a heart problem, he sent off fifteen cents and three candy bar wrappers for a magic kit in a TV ad. Although he became a high school Latin teacher, he kept practicing magic in his off hours. Jillette loved jugglers and magic acts on TV, but he hated magicians who pretended to have supernatural powers. He favored performers like the Amazing Randi who approached magic as an amusing game to deceive people. "Early on, Teller said to me that magic was essentially an intellectual art form which, when you picture the kind of [jerks] that do magic, sounds like an insane thing to say," notes Jillette. "Can you do magic without insulting the audience? Can you do magic that is intellectually satisfying? It is those questions, rather than the magic itself, that fascinates me."[12]

> "Can you do magic without insulting the audience? Can you do magic that is intellectually satisfying? It is those questions, rather than the magic itself, that fascinates me."[12]
>
> —Penn Jillette

Eventually Jillette went to the Ringling Brothers Barnum and Bailey Clown College and learned wire walking and juggling. He was homeless and drifting when he met Teller shortly thereafter through a mutual friend named Wier Chrisimer in August 1975. For several years the three had an act called Asparagus Valley Cultural Society, which played at the Phoenix Theater in San Francisco, California. The act was equal parts magic show and silly comedy routine. Chrisimer helped his partners create some set pieces that would become staples for Penn & Teller, such as Teller's celebrated shadow-flower trick. Despite personalities that clashed and a few unpleasant confrontations—particularly in their early years together—Jillette and Teller realized they made an effective team. "Teller and I never got along," Penn admits. "We never had a cuddly friendship. It was a very cold, calculated relationship where we thought we do better stuff together than we do separately."[13] Jillette was a natural at talking to the audience, and Teller had always performed as a mute, discovering that his silence helped tame unruly crowds.

Moving to New York, the duo got strong reviews for an off-Broadway show they wrote called *Mrs. Lonsberry's Séance of Horror*. Then it was back to the West Coast and a successful run at the LA Stage Company Theatre in Hollywood. Billed as the Bad Boys of Magic, Penn & Teller increasingly focused on effects that were edgy, violent, and even shocking, although always with an underlying sense of humor. In 1985 they starred in another off-Broadway show and also appeared in their first TV special on PBS, *Penn & Teller Go Public*, which won an Emmy award. They made frequent guest appearances on TV talk shows, comedies, and dramas throughout the late 1980s and 1990s. They even played street magicians scamming people at three-card Monte, a con game utilizing playing cards, in a music video for the rap act Run DMC. Their shows and tours drew rave reviews, earning them a reputation as America's hippest magic act. In 2001 Penn & Teller began performing six nights a week at the Rio Hotel in Las Vegas, a run that continues to this day.

> "Our point was, we are the ones that the magicians hate. So if you don't like those other magicians, you should come see us."[14]
>
> —Penn Jillette

A Different Kind of Magic Show

One reason for Penn & Teller's success is their determination to present a different kind of magic show. By the 1980s, when the duo first began performing together, magic was considered mostly for children, and magicians were thought to be condescending to their audience. Penn & Teller rebelled against all that. They aimed to reach a wider audience of adults by appealing to

The renowned and spectacularly successful magical duo Penn & Teller seem oddly matched as performers. Penn (left) is tall, brash, and opinionated; Teller (right) is short, quiet, and reflective.

people's intelligence and also by breaking some of the hallowed rules of magic. For example, Penn would sometimes tell the audience how a certain trick was done. This brought howls of protest from their fellow magicians, whose nasty quotes made good publicity to promote the act. "Our point was, we are the ones that the magicians hate," says Penn. "So if you don't like those other magicians, you should come see us. Which was really our point, but it was being said in a whimsical, theoretical way."[14]

The team loves to demystify magic, as if the tricks are really beautifully simple, and then go several steps further to astonish the audience all over again. On one TV appearance, they explained their Man in a Box routine, in which Teller's head, hands, and legs seem to be in separate boxes. First they performed the trick with regular boxes and then with transparent boxes that showed how Teller slithered around beneath the stage in order to pop up in the separate boxes and create the effect. "What Teller

Shadow Flowers and Copyright Law

Magicians through the years have often adapted or stolen each other's best material. Yet one of Teller's solo tricks is so distinctive that he won a lawsuit against an imitator who performed it. The trick, called Shadows, has been a staple of Penn & Teller's act for four decades. It consists of a spotlight and a bud vase containing a rose. The light is trained on the rose, throwing its shadow onto a white paper screen a short distance behind it. Teller approaches with a large knife and proceeds to cut the leaves and petals—not of the actual rose but of its shadow. As each shadow petal is cut, the corresponding petal of the real rose is severed from the stem and falls to the ground. The trick never fails to mesmerize an audience. As Penn has said, "No one knows how Shadows is done, and no one will ever figure it out."

Recognizing the trick's value, Teller registered Shadows with the US Copyright Office in 1983. He included drawings of the trick—but not its secret—in his application. A few years ago Gerard Dogge, a Belgian magician, posted a YouTube video of himself performing The Rose & Her Shadow, a similar illusion. Teller sued Dogge for copyright infringement and won. In March 2014 the judge in the case ruled that while a magic trick cannot be copyrighted, the pantomime act that goes along with it can. The result: Teller's unique artistry was upheld in a court of law.

Quoted in Eriq Gardner, "Teller Wins Lawsuit over Copied Magic Trick Performance," *Hollywood Reporter*, March 21, 2014. www.hollywoodreporter.com.

and I would do is we would write methods that really were fascinating, and then give those away as though that's the way all magic was done," says Penn. "So the big lie in the Penn & Teller show is, we go out in the first or second trick and show you how a trick is done. And what we have taught you then is, this is the level of cleverness and beauty that all our tricks have, and we don't tell you the rest. And the rest of them are ugly."[15]

The so-called ugly tricks Penn refers to require lots of hard work. The pair insists that is what separates them from their competitors. They might work off and on for six years on a trick that takes three minutes. They will perform it again and again with helpers scrutinizing each complicated step from several spots in the auditorium, looking for a mistake that would tip off an audience. Only when the mechanics of a trick are flawless—when they can perform it with apparent casualness—do they add it to the act.

An Undercurrent of Violence

Another hallmark of Penn & Teller's act is an undercurrent of violence or cruelty that always seems about to erupt. Much of the duo's comedy is based on Penn's callous treatment of the silent, childlike Teller. For example, Penn will strap Teller into a straitjacket, suspend him upside down over spikes or bear traps, or prepare to dismember him with a chainsaw. In one early routine Penn locked Teller into a tank filled with water and had his breathing tube snatched away while musing to the audience about Houdini's reported record of holding his breath for four minutes. Then, while a female assistant kept time with a stopwatch, Penn pretended to ignore Teller's predicament while he focused on a difficult card trick. After five minutes, Penn would mention in an offhand way that Teller was certainly brain-dead by now. With

Teller flinches as props shatter during a Penn & Teller performance. One hallmark of their act is an undercurrent of violence or cruelty—usually directed by Penn toward Teller.

the audience chuckling a bit uneasily as Penn searched through his deck of cards, Teller, still alive and breathing, was revealed to have the marked card inside his scuba mask.

One popular bit of stage violence by the team harkened back to the great nineteenth-century French magician Robert-Houdin. Stationed at opposite ends of the stage behind identical panes of glass, Penn and Teller would each fire a .357 Magnum handgun at the other and catch the other's bullet in his mouth. It was a rare instance of equal-opportunity mayhem, with Teller taking a potshot at his partner.

Friends Who Don't Socialize

The way Penn mistreats and even threatens to maim Teller onstage gives the impression that the two barely get along. And Penn often says in interviews that he and Teller don't spend time together away from work. But this is another example of the duo's habit of misdirection. Of their relationship Penn says, "It's entirely intellectual and is not in any way cuddly or friendly. That having been said, over 39 years, he's clearly my best friend. And for any important thing that happens, like the birth of my children, the death of our parents, any sort of real problem, we go to each other."[16]

The magicians reside only a few miles apart outside Las Vegas, Nevada. Until recently Penn lived in a huge, rather eccentric house in the Mojave Desert. The house, which he called the Slammer, included rooms in primary colors, indoor slides and fire-station poles, a mug-shot camera for visitors, a parlor decorated with classic playing cards, and a recording studio. Penn married his wife Emily in 2004 and they have two children, Zolten and Moxie CrimeFighter. Teller lives alone on a hilltop in a large maze of a mansion. His home is like a playhouse, with hidden doors, mirrored walls, tables that scream, a coffin, complete with skeleton inside, and a bear sculpture that talks and does card tricks for visitors. "Like much of my life, this house is a reflection of everything I wanted back when I was 12," says Teller. "I love this house because it's honest. If you see a floor that looks like concrete, that's because it is concrete. But, ah, on the other hand, nothing is what it seems."[17] In his spare time he directs stage plays—his *Macbeth* included witches that actually vanished—and collects memorabilia related to Houdini, whom he and Penn both revere as a master.

Some of Penn and Teller's differences are reflected in their work. Unlike Penn, who loves tricks with an intellectual basis, Teller focuses on the beauty and emotional effect of magic. Most of the duo's bits are harsh and ironic, but Teller performs some tricks that are more endearing. For example, he will snip away at the shadow of a rose, causing a real rose to shed its petals. Or he will make a pet out of a red ball, leading it to jump through hoops and chase along at his heels like a devoted spaniel. "Doing beautiful things is its own reward," says Teller. "If you do something that you're proud of, that someone else understands, that is a thing of beauty that wasn't there before—you can't beat that."[18]

> "If you do something that you're proud of, that someone else understands, that is a thing of beauty that wasn't there before—you can't beat that."[18]
>
> —Teller

Professional Skeptics

Penn & Teller's success as master magicians has led them into a parallel career as professional skeptics. They come by their skepticism naturally, both being atheists, libertarians, and devotees of science. Like their hero Houdini, Penn & Teller enjoy exposing frauds and cranks not only in the world of magic but in any area of life. Their original targets were magicians who claimed to possess special powers. "The people who claim these powers are liars, cheaters, swindlers, rip-offs," says Penn. "And the tricks themselves are evil, immoral—and I know how to do them all!"[19] Beginning in 2003 the team hosted a cable TV series in which they set out to debunk fake science, popular fads and misconceptions, paranormal beliefs, and other false ideas. In their typical blunt style—the name of the series is a vulgar word for nonsense—they dealt with alien abductions, alternative medicine, organic foods, and ESP. At the end of each episode Penn would summarize the pair's problems with a certain belief and why it is harmful. The

Penn & Teller's *Fool Us*

Penn & Teller earned their nickname as the Bad Boys of Magic by occasionally revealing the secret behind one of their tricks. For example, they sometimes perform the perennial cups-and-balls trick with clear plastic cups to show where the sleight of hand comes in. At times the duo seems to be saying to the audience: *See how easy it is to fool you?* And then they proceed to toss off a more complex illusion that is genuinely mystifying.

This background makes the magicians ideal for the magic competition show called *Penn & Teller: Fool Us*. The show features performers who attempt to fool Penn & Teller as to how they do their tricks. Among the acts have been close-up coin and card magic, mind reading, quick-change costume switches, and escape tricks. Following each trick Penn and Teller confer, drawing on their vast knowledge of stage magic. Sometimes they resort to professional jargon like "Tamariz" or "McCombical decks" as shorthand for the secret behind a trick. In the end Penn & Teller are rarely stumped. They can explain the mechanics of a trick in plain language—while usually withholding one or two important keys. Still, certain magicians continue to fume that the duo are revealing trade secrets. So, is it wrong to give away a trick? "No it's not!" says Teller. "The person who wrote the magic book that got you started in magic gave away a trick. Was that an evil deed? No!"

Quoted in Kevin Pang, "Penn and Teller Are Revealing How Their Magic Tricks Are Done—and It's O.K.," *Vanity Fair*, September 21, 2015. www.vanityfair.com.

show won eleven Emmy awards. In a similar scientific vein, Penn & Teller collaborated on *Tim's Vermeer*, a 2013 documentary that examines how the great seventeenth-century Dutch painter Johannes Vermeer might have used a camera obscura, an early optical instrument, to create his masterpieces.

In the course of revealing the secrets behind so many deceptions, Penn & Teller have made their own job as magicians that much harder. Audiences are now primed to be skeptics themselves, to scrutinize each trick with a wary eye. Still, the team always rises to the challenge. One new trick involves an air-powered nail gun. As he fires nails into a board, Penn explains how he has memorized the pattern of nails and blanks in the gun's magazine. He then rapidly alternates between shooting nails into the board and shooting blanks into the palm of his hand—or toward Teller's crotch. The audience's laughter becomes a little hesitant as Penn seems to have trouble recalling the exact pattern of nails and blanks. He assures the crowd that he and Teller would never attempt anything really dangerous onstage. That would be immoral. It would make the people complicit in a risky enterprise. Meanwhile the audience members wince at each shot from that nail gun.

CHAPTER 3

Ricky Jay

Deborah Baron, a Hollywood screenwriter, has a favorite story about her friend, the magician Ricky Jay. It is New Year's Eve and a dozen guests, including Jay, have gathered at Baron's home for a dinner party. After midnight the group assembles around the coffee table to watch Jay perform his specialty: close-up card magic. Jay has small hands for a magician, but his fingers work miracles and playing cards fit snugly in his palms. He adroitly dazzles the guests with a number of choice effects and prepares to call it an evening. Then a guest named Mort pipes up. "Come on, Ricky. Why don't you do something truly amazing?"[20] Jay gives the man a look for a moment. With his beard, craggy features, and hooded eyes, Jay can seem imposing, like the lowlife characters he sometimes portrays in movies. He then tells Mort to name a card, any card. Mort names the three of hearts. Jay shuffles the deck, grips it in his right hand, and sprays the cards the length of the table toward an open wine bottle. Jay asks Mort to name his card again, and again he says the three of hearts. Jay tells him to look inside the bottle. Mort finds, curled inside the bottle's neck, the three of hearts. Baron and her guests stare in disbelief. They are convinced that Ricky Jay is the best in the world at what he does.

Learning from His Grandfather

Ricky Jay has been astonishing audiences with close-up magic for decades. Ricky Jay was born Richard Jay Potash in Brooklyn, New York, on an unrecorded day in 1948. His family moved to Elizabeth, New Jersey, while he was very young. Jay was raised in a middle-class Jewish household that he rarely mentions. At least, he rarely speaks seriously about his childhood. "My father was the Formica King of Long Island," he once told a reporter from *People* magazine, "and my mother was the daughter of a Bengal Lancer in India."[21]

As a child he loved games, particularly chess and baseball, and he also wrote constantly. But his first love was magic. His interest came from his grandfather, Max Katz, a certified public accountant, calligrapher, billiards player, math enthusiast, and devoted amateur magician. Max served for a time as president of the Society of American Magicians. He was also the only member of the family who loved Ricky for himself. Jay notes that Max taught all his grandchildren how to do magic tricks, but Jay was the only one who got hooked on the activity. Like Max, Jay learned to pursue his interests by taking lessons from the best available people and then expanding on that knowledge.

He began practicing at home with the clichéd top hat and magic wand. He was four years old when he first performed in public, multiplying little coffee creamers at a meeting of his grandfather's magic group. At age seven, he turned a guinea pig into a dove on a local TV show, which led to a story in the *Newark Sunday News*. Young Ricky Potash was photographed holding what would become the key to his future—a deck of playing cards—but he told the reporter he certainly did not want to be a professional magician.

Nonetheless, at fourteen he began playing around town as Tricky Ricky, a magician in a bullfighter jacket and penciled-in sideburns. His specialty was causing a cane to float in the air. He also bused into Manhattan to take magic lessons from the Great Slydini, one of Max's clients and a master of close-up effects. While there, he would check out the nightclubs in Greenwich Village. "Most of my classmates had this strange psychological barrier about going into the city, but I would go see [jazz musicians] Roland Kirk, [Thelonius] Monk, [John] Coltrane," says Jay. "I remember seeing [comedian] Richard Pryor at the Cafe Wha. And of course the magicians."[22] He loved to hang out at the cluttered magic shop of Al Flosso, another sleight-of-hand veteran, and comb through old books and posters from bygone eras.

Ricky Jay dazzles audiences with an astounding array of card tricks. The beard, craggy features, and hooded eyes add to Jay's stage persona.

A Hippie Magician

After Max died, Jay struck out on his own. He tried college and various ways of making money—bartending, selling encyclopedias, even gambling at cards—but kept returning to magic. Billed as Ricky Jay, he appeared on *The Tonight Show* in the early 1970s, which led to higher-paying club dates across the country. He developed the persona of a hippie magician, with long hair, a flowing beard, fringed vests, flowery shirts, and bell-bottoms. He toured and played clubs with some of the biggest acts in music, including Ike and Tina Turner, Herbie Hancock, and Emmylou Harris. Jay also developed his own comic style of patter, employing fancy language in a droll manner. "The thing Ricky had that I'd never before seen in a magician was charm," says TV writer Tracy Newman, who dated Jay for a time. "At McCabe's [a music club], he was doing improvisational patter. He had his stuff down so well he was just free. He had the guts to bring people onstage and really play with them, instead of having to be so careful that they might see something that would cause him to blow what he was trying to do. He was very casual, but his language had a Shakespearean feel."[23]

> "[Ricky] had the guts to bring people onstage and really play with them, instead of having to be so careful that they might see something that would cause him to blow what he was trying to do."[23]
>
> —Tracy Newman, a TV writer who used to date Jay

Jay made his home in Los Angeles, mainly to be close to Dai Vernon, a master of close-up magic who was known as the Professor. When not touring, he would spend hours with Vernon and another sleight-of-hand expert, Charlie Miller. He loved their stories about the old days and their devotion to the art of magic. Vernon and Miller would let him in on the secrets behind some of their tricks and stubbornly withhold others. Despite his long hair and wild clothes, Jay was a traditionalist in many ways who sought, like his mentors, to preserve the secrets of his craft. He worked obsessively day after day—manipulating coins and cards and cups and balls—to make himself a more skillful magician and illusionist.

The Magic Castle

When Jay first moved to the West Coast, he would spend hours listening to stories by veteran magicians. They would often meet at the Magic Castle, a members-only club in Hollywood, California. The club, which dates to 1959, resides in a large frame-and-plaster house originally built in 1909. Members of this celebrated club have included all types of magicians, both amateur and professional, from sleight-of-hand artists to mind readers to masters of large-scale illusions. It was while hanging out with his mentor, Dai Vernon, at the Magic Castle that Jay learned important lessons about scrutinizing details in order to be a better performer. One night he and Vernon spent two hours just watching people put on their coats. Vernon pointed out how each person did it a little differently.

Today, however, Jay avoids the Magic Castle. For years he has viewed it as mostly a haven for second-raters, gossips, and thieves. Jay also refuses to perform for other magicians, a policy that has led some to dismiss him as an elitist. Such criticisms amuse him more than anything. He knows how much work it takes to develop a routine for the stage, and he has no intention of spilling his secrets for those seeking a shortcut to success. The idea of magic tricks being explained on the Internet or in TV specials appalls him. The old magicians that used to frequent the Magic Castle would guard their signature tricks with their lives, and Jay still swears by their example.

Card Handling as an Art Form

Other professional magicians are amazed at Jay's technical mastery of close-up magic—what they call his *chops*. He developed an act that combined these chops with droll, irreverent comedy. He would open by fanning a deck of cards in each hand to make perfect semicircles. He would ask people in the audience to name a card and then produce that particular card with lightning speed. Often he would demonstrate a unique skill: throwing playing cards. Jay can toss a card outward 6 feet (1.8 m) in the air and make it boomerang back to him. He also can throw an ordinary playing card 90 miles per hour (145 kph) and make it travel almost 200 feet (61 m)—stunts that earned him a spot in the *Guinness Book of World Records*. At ten paces he can pierce the rind of a watermelon, making the card stick there like a dagger. Then he would proceed to the Laughing Card Trick. After first showing the audience his empty hands, Jay would repeatedly snatch a card from nowhere—each a jack of spades—and place it between his lips. With each card Jay would cackle more and more maniacally. He did this four times, finally removing the cards from his mouth to reveal they were now the four aces.

Eventually he would move on to what many peers consider his masterpiece: the Four Queens. At the beginning of this effect, Jay effortlessly pops out the four queens from the middle of a deck of cards, trick enough for some magicians. He groups each queen with three numbered cards dealt face down on top of it. Jay pretends each queen is trapped and under siege from her three suitors. As he explains to the audience in Victorian language: "Ladies and gentlemen, as you have seen, I have taken advantage of these tenderly nurtured and unsophisticated young ladies by placing them in positions extremely galling to their aristocratic sensibilities."[24] He then turns over each group to reveal four numbered cards, with the final group shown to be the four reunited queens. Michael Weber, Jay's business partner, recalls seeing him perform the Four Queens on a network TV special. "It was a transcendent moment in popular magic," he says. "Ricky had attitude, presentation, humor, and chops. Everybody was talking about that show. It was one of those times when all the elements of his talent were so self-evidently on display that even the people who could never before get it finally got it."[25] After witnessing Jay's performance of the Four Queens at a lecture at UCLA, his mentor the Professor told him he had restored dignity to the art of magic.

> "[Jay's TV special] was one of those times when all the elements of his talent were so self-evidently on display that even the people who could never before get it finally got it."[25]
>
> —Michael Weber, Jay's business partner

Pride in His Craft

Jay prides himself on his attention to the details of his craft. To him, sleight-of-hand masters are shortchanged in the public mind compared to the gaudy entertainers who do large-scale illusions. Among his biggest influences are friends who are not even professional magicians, just inspired amateurs. Jay loves to spend time with these fellow sleight-of-hand enthusiasts. He insists that many of them have world-class skills, despite never having made a dime from performing magic. Most caught the magic bug in childhood just as he did and have been hooked ever since. As Jay explains,

> Like every art form, there are jealousies and angers and competitiveness in magic. But there's camaraderie among magicians, whether you perform it for a living or you're an enthusiast. I don't think that's as common among writers, or comedians; I think it's one of the things that makes magic unique, this love of it that crosses the boundary between professionals and certain amateurs. Because they're amateurs in the right sense of the word, they are people who do it simply for their love of it.[26]

Jay also loves to research the history of magic. He gets many of his best ideas from old books on the subject. Starting with some discovery or small principle, he will then develop it into a whole theatrical presentation. He often works on a single trick for months or even years without showing anyone the result. His goal is a perfect mix of originality, surprise, and clarity. He is at pains to get the total effect and the accompanying patter just right before he will even consider presenting a new trick onstage. Such obsessive labor partly explains his outrage when a second-rate magician steals one of his routines. He compares it to someone coming to his house for dinner and leaving with his TV.

> "I think it's one of the things that makes magic unique, this love of it that crosses the boundary between professionals and certain amateurs."[26]
>
> —Ricky Jay

A Diverse Career

Jay's zealously guarded bag of tricks has helped him enjoy a diverse career in show business. In 1987 he appeared in David Mamet's first film, *House of Games*, as a rich Texas poker player who has a *tell*—an involuntary gesture that reveals when he has a good hand. Jay went on to appear in several more of Mamet's movies, most of which involve cons and scams. In 1989 he performed close-up magic and mused about eccentric entertainers of the past in *Learned Pigs & Fireproof Women*, a network TV special based on a book he wrote. In 1994 he starred in *Ricky Jay and His 52 Assistants*, a one-man show directed by Mamet. (The fifty-two assistants referred to a deck of playing cards.) The award-winning show eventually traveled to theaters worldwide.

In 2002 Jay and Mamet collaborated again on *Ricky Jay: On the Stem*, a theater show based on the con artist's trade that ran for seven months in New York City. Mamet also directed 2009's

Jay (right) appears in a scene from Redbelt, *a 2008 movie that was written and directed by David Mamet. Jay and Mamet have collaborated on several movies, most of which revolve around cons and scams.*

Ricky Jay: A Rogue's Gallery, in which Jay performed his classic routines and regaled audiences with stories from his career. Jay has appeared in several movies by directors other than Mamet, including the 2006 film *The Prestige*, about a pair of nineteenth-century magicians feuding over stage illusions.

Dexterity with the written word is another of Jay's talents. With his encyclopedic knowledge of magic, he was the obvious choice to write the article on conjuring for the *Encyclopaedia Britannica*. In the early 2000s he wrote scripts for the cable western drama *Deadwood*, and also took the role of a craps player and con man on the show. He has produced books on the history of magic and on the sort of oddball sideshow characters he loves. He also wrote *Dice: Deception, Fate & Rotten Luck*, a look at dice and craps hustlers through the ages. For the latter book he included photographs of classic dice—loaded, shaved, and otherwise adapted for cheating—from his own vast collection. His home is like a museum devoted to magic and magicians, second-tier show-business figures, and games of chance, with thousands of books, posters, handbills, postcards, and memorabilia accumulated over decades. He likes nothing better than to spend weekend afternoons with his wife, Chrisann, strolling through flea markets and used bookstores in search of rare finds.

Everyday Magic

Few days are ordinary in Ricky Jay's world. His sleight-of-hand wizardry can transform a humdrum situation into something amazing and memorable. An example comes from Suzie MacKenzie, a British journalist who several years ago was working with the BBC on a documentary about Jay. The director and Jay were at odds over Jay performing an effect first done by a magician from the early 1900s, Max Malini. (Malini is one of Jay's favorite magicians, partly because his real name was the same as Jay's grandfather—Max Katz.) At a dinner party Malini had famously spun a coin on the table, covered it with a woman's hat he had borrowed, and raised the hat to disclose a large block of ice. MacKenzie, who knew Jay could be cantankerous when crossed, warily agreed to have lunch with the magician and dis-

On the Stem

With his quick-fingered ability to manipulate a deck of cards, Ricky Jay would seem to be the perfect card-game hustler. When asked if he has ever bamboozled other players for money, Jay smiles but refuses to say. Certainly the intricacies of fooling people are key to his livelihood, and he likes nothing better than exploring the techniques of the classic hustlers and con artists. This pastime led to his off-Broadway hit show *Ricky Jay: On the Stem*. The show paid tribute to the hucksters, swindlers, and confidence men who decades ago made their living along Broadway—called "the stem," in hipster language.

The evening would always include the effortless fleecing of a tourist. Jay would invite a male member of the audience to come on stage and hand him a credit card. Then he would put the credit card in a small yellow envelope. Jay would have the man slip the envelope into his wallet, wrap it in a rubber band, and put it in his pocket. After a pause, Jay would ask the man to check his wallet again. The man would take out the wallet, remove the rubber band, and open the envelope. Inside was a card that said "Brooklyn Bridge Ownership." Then a messenger would hurry down from the back of the theater and hand the man his credit card. As Jay admits, "The con—the big con, especially—is an entire theatrical orchestration for an audience of one. It's both lovely and diabolical at the same time."

Quoted in Neil A. Grauer, "The Wizard of Odd," *Smithsonian*, June 2004. www.smithsonianmag.com.

cuss the matter at a restaurant on Sunset Boulevard in Los Angeles. It was a scorching day, the freeway was jammed with cars, and Jay missed his exit in the traffic crush. When they finally arrived at the restaurant, hot and weary, MacKenzie noticed it was stuffy inside from the sun pouring through the large plate glass windows. They got a table and Jay idly began to describe Malini's trick while he examined the menu. Then, as MacKenzie recalls, he suddenly lifted his menu to reveal behind it an enormous block of ice, already beginning to melt. MacKenzie was speechless. She actually burst into tears at the wonder of it. Touched by her reaction, Jay told her, "That's what I do for a living."[27]

CHAPTER 4

David Copperfield

The Statue of Liberty, located on Liberty Island in New York Harbor, stands 305 feet (93 m) tall from the bottom of its base to the tip of its torch. It weighs 225 tons (204 metric tons). The construction of the colossal statue from its disassembled pieces is still considered one of the major engineering feats of the late 1800s. For a live TV special in 1983, the magician David Copperfield prepares to make the statue vanish. At night an audience is seated on the island, 200 feet (61 m) from the statue. Two scaffolding towers have been raised in front of the statue, and helicopters hover overhead to record the event. Surrounding the statue is a circle of lights shining upon it. A large radar setup registers the statue as a green blip in the center of the screen.

At Copperfield's direction a huge curtain rises up between the pillars, shielding the statue from the audience's view. On the telecast, a Bach oratorio plays in the background to emphasize the grandeur of the event. Copperfield raises his arms and gestures for the curtain to be lowered. Behind it there is nothing but blackness. A pair of searchlights crisscrosses the area where the statue stood just moments before. The statue has vanished from the radar screen. The view from a helicopter reveals an empty circle of lights. The audience gasps and jumps up to applaud. One man admits that were he at home watching on TV he would be skeptical, but he has just witnessed the disappearance with his own eyes. Shortly thereafter Copperfield orders the curtain raised again, then lowers it to reveal the statue fully lit and restored to its place. David Copperfield's Statue of Liberty performance becomes the new standard for large-scale illusions in the field of magic.

Overcoming Shyness by Performing

The master illusionist David Copperfield was born David Seth Kotkin on September 16, 1956, in Metuchen, New Jersey. His father, Hyman, was the son of Jewish immigrants from Russia and ran a men's clothing store. His mother, Rebecca, came to the United States from Israel and worked as an insurance adjuster. An only child and very shy, David practiced to be a ventriloquist. At age eight he went to the magic counter at the Manhattan department store Macy's to purchase a ventriloquist dummy. He was fascinated by a clerk demonstrating a vanishing coin trick on a little wooden board. David ended up buying the trick, and suddenly he had to have more. "I remember looking through the New York phone book for a magic store, and I found Louis Tannen Magic," he says. "I went there, the elevator door opened, and I knew my life was changing. Everyone knows that feeling, like you've walked into heaven. Man, you walked in, and you just went, 'This is it!'"[28]

> "I went [to the magic store], the elevator door opened, and I knew my life was changing. Everyone knows that feeling, like you've walked into heaven. Man, you walked in, and you just went, 'This is it!'"[28]
>
> —David Copperfield

David abandoned ventriloquism, which was no great loss because he was not very good at it anyway. He began to accumulate the classic tools of the stage magician, from the endless scarves up his sleeve to the rubber balls that seemed to vanish and reappear in little cups. He became obsessive about his new interest, spending hours alone honing his skills. His ability to perform crowd-pleasing tricks helped him overcome his insecurity around strangers. For neighborhood shows and parties, he took the name Davino the Boy Magician. David was twelve and already an experienced conjurer and entertainer when he gained membership in the Society of American Magicians, becoming the youngest ever to do so.

Word quickly got around about the fabulous young magician from Metuchen. As a teenager David maintained a busy performing schedule along with his schoolwork. He discovered that magic skills not only broke the ice with strangers; they also helped him attract the interest of girls. By age sixteen, his shyness was mostly conquered. That year New York University named him an adjunct professor and had him teach a course on the art of magic. The expert magician at the lectern was younger than his students.

The Magic Man and TV Specials

At age eighteen, David parlayed his magic skills into a much larger opportunity than his teaching job. He was chosen to play the lead in a new musical comedy called The Magic Man. The show, which opened in 1975 in Chicago to sparkling reviews, gave him the opportunity to act, sing, and display his talents in stage magic. He also designed all the show's magical effects. The Magic Man went on to have the longest run of any musical in Chicago history. Those daily performances in front of a live audience raised David's level of confidence to new heights. When the show finally closed, he was ready to accept a new challenge.

> "I really wanted to tell stories and take the audience on a journey, and not have any stereotypical magic items in hand."[29]
>
> —David Copperfield

Moving back to New York, he developed a new magic act that drew upon the things he loved most in show business. These included the elegance of Hollywood musicals and the stylish swagger of singer Frank Sinatra's performing style. "I really wanted to tell stories and take the audience on a journey," he says, "and not have any stereotypical magic items in hand."[29] At a friend's suggestion, he took

David Copperfield appears to levitate his assistant during a 1985 performance. A master illusionist, Copperfield set a new standard for large-scale illusions in the field of magic.

the name David Copperfield, from the lead character in a novel by the nineteenth-century English author Charles Dickens. Tall and slim with dark hair and eyes, David had the look of a film star. He was intent on bringing a new kind of drama and glamour to the magic trade.

In 1977 the national TV audience discovered Copperfield when he introduced the ABC network's fall TV lineup in a number of clever promotional spots that featured him performing magic tricks and illusions. The exposure led rival network CBS to hire the young magician for a series of TV specials, each more daring and ambitious than the last. The specials consistently won high ratings and critical praise, not to mention twenty-one Emmy awards. As TV historian J. Walker notes:

> Very few television stars can be said to have become synonymous with their art forms. Even the very best among the best have competitors, challengers to the throne, an up-and-coming threat on another network. But for quite a long time, starting in the late 1970s and continuing into the early '90s, when you thought of magic on television, there was only one name that came to mind: David Copperfield. Copperfield *was* magic in that era, a time when his almost-yearly *The Magic of David Copperfield* specials were anticipated, important television events.[30]

Dazzling Large-Scale Illusions

Copperfield's early specials were like variety shows, with guest stars and musical acts. He would alternate between performing smaller sleight-of-hand tricks, during which he would pepper the audience with wisecracks and corny jokes, and more lavish illusions, complete with dramatic lighting, smoke machines, and rock music. To keep viewers coming back, Copperfield began to devise ever more dazzling large-scale illusions. Each show would culminate in one spectacular effect. For example, he made a 7-ton (6.4-metric ton) Learjet disappear. He levitated over the Grand Canyon. He stepped through the Great Wall of China like a ghost. And, in a 1983 special, he produced what many consider his most memorable effect, causing the Statue of Liberty to vanish and then reappear.

Not since Houdini had a single magician captured the American public's fancy so completely. He even dabbled in Houdini's specialty, escaping from a

> "For quite a long time, starting in the late 1970s and continuing into the early '90s, when you thought of magic on television, there was only one name that came to mind: David Copperfield."[30]
>
> —J. Walker, TV historian

A Deadly Plunge

David Copperfield presents himself as a supremely confident performer, but he concedes that one trick unnerved him like no other. For the finale of his last TV special in 1990, he planned a risky escape to avoid plunging over Niagara Falls. In later interviews Copperfield admitted he thought the trick might well kill him.

As with his other large-scale effects, he prepared meticulously. He was to be shackled hand and foot and strapped into a steel box attached to a large raft, which would then be set afire. The raft would be launched toward the falls on steel ramps. Copperfield had to escape from his shackles and restraints and leap aboard a Jet Ski just before the raft went over. Signs of trouble appeared with the first run-through. When crew members lowered the steel ramps into the water, the power of the rushing current shredded the steel and crossbeams like spaghetti. A stuntman hired to stand in for Copperfield during preparations refused to do it. "I remember going to my hotel room every night and dreaming how I was going to die," says Copperfield. "It was really, really horrible."

On the appointed day, the TV audience watched as the raft tumbled over the falls with the magician still aboard, there was a breathless pause, and then a helicopter rose from below with the magician suspended from it by a rope. Exhilarated by the experience, Copperfield says, "It was glorious, and I was like, 'Can I do it again?'"

Quoted in Stan Allen, "David Copperfield Discusses Hospitalization, Brush with Death and More," *Las Vegas Sun*, September 28, 2012. http://lasvegassun.com.

straitjacket while hanging upside down from burning ropes ten stories above a bed of steel spikes. The sheer size of his tricks seemed made for the age of TV. People tuned in simply to see if Copperfield could top himself once again. His 1992 special, subtitled *Flying—Live the Dream*, may have been his greatest production. The show focused on the human dream of flight, ending with Copperfield willing himself to fly above the theater stage to the astonishment of the audience. "The [flying] illusion itself is quite impressive on its own," says Walker, "but even more so by the way the entire hour builds to the moment when he finally leaves the ground."[31] Copperfield had learned how to give his specials a feeling of dramatic tension and release, just like the Hollywood movies he loved.

Creating his illusions required great patience and meticulous preparation. Copperfield became known for not cutting corners. "It takes at least 2 years to develop illusions and some of them take even longer," he has said. "I love to challenge my team and myself by pushing the envelope and working on new methods and ideas. I don't always take the easiest route. Sometimes, the ultimate solution requires months of brainstorming, miniatures and mock-ups, and testing just to make an idea a reality."[32]

From Broadway to Las Vegas

Despite his hard work, by the mid-1990s Copperfield had begun to repeat himself. His later TV specials lacked the old spark of inspiration. In 1996 he teamed with film director Francis Ford Coppola to create a new Broadway show, *Dreams and Nightmares*. Once again he was performing every night before a live audience. The show quickly became a runaway success, setting a Broadway record for most tickets sold in one week.

In 2001 Copperfield returned to TV with a special titled *Tornado of Fire*. In the years since his last TV appearance, the landscape of the magic business had changed. The FOX Network had presented four controversial specials of its own, in a series called *Breaking the Magician's Code: Magic's Biggest Secrets Finally Revealed*. Val Valentino, a Las Vegas performer disguised as the Masked Magician, demonstrated how some of the most popular stage illusions were done—including a few of Copperfield's staples. At the same time a new breed of so-called street magicians had arrived. A brash young performer like David Blaine chose to take his sleight-of-hand talents out on the street, mystifying strangers with close-up tricks recorded by a handheld camera. By comparison Copperfield's lavish illusions seemed old-fashioned. *Tornado of Fire*'s climax, in which Copperfield, wrapped in a flame-retardant foil, stood in a wind tunnel and endured a barrage of flamethrowers, failed to impress. It was his last TV special.

Nonetheless Copperfield rebounded. He took his stage act to Las Vegas, the perfect venue for his elegant style and reliable effects. Whereas younger illusionists like Blaine and Criss Angel generate more excitement today among critics, Copperfield can console himself with his status as one of the richest entertainers in the world. In addition to his Las Vegas run, he has made several world tours. According to his website, no other solo performer in history has sold more tickets.

Project Magic and Other Interests

Copperfield's financial success has enabled him to take on many new challenges. His personal favorite is Project Magic, the inspiration for which dates to the early 1980s. At that time Copperfield

Copperfield teaches a magic trick to a twelve-year-old girl during a Project Magic event in Toronto, Canada. The renowned illusionist created the program to assist physical therapy patients with dexterity, coordination, and thinking skills.

How to Make the Statue of Liberty Disappear

Obeying the unwritten code of magicians, David Copperfield will never reveal how he performed his most famous illusion: making the Statue of Liberty vanish in front of a live audience. However, aside from a few details, most experts agree about how the trick was accomplished. As with many illusions, the key was misdirection—making the audience look elsewhere.

The viewpoint of the live audience, as well as of the camera, was through the two pillars that framed the statue. When the curtain rose up to the arch connecting the pillars, the statue was out of sight. At that point a rotating table silently shifted the audience and the curtained pillars a few degrees to the side. Thus when the curtain was lowered, the statue was no longer visible between the pillars. The audience and the camera were now looking at empty space to the side of the statue. A second circle of lights made it look as though the statue was gone. The sweeping searchlights showed nothing. And the radar blip representing the statue was also gone—since the radar screen was a fake prop to begin with.

To make the statue reappear, Copperfield had only to raise the curtain and then rotate the platform back to its original location. Voilà! The Statue of Liberty was back in place, and the onlookers reacted with amazement. Experts disagree on whether the live audience actually was in on the trick. Certainly David Copperfield will never tell.

was corresponding with another magician by mail. When he received a press clipping from the man, Copperfield was surprised to learn from a photograph that the man was in a wheelchair. The man had never mentioned his condition and did not consider it any hindrance to his career in magic. Copperfield wondered if learning magic could help others overcome physical disabilities and boost their self-confidence.

He took his idea to therapists at the Daniel Freeman Memorial Hospital in Inglewood, California, one of the top rehabilitation centers in the country. They recognized at once the potential for using magic in physical therapy. Learning to perform sleight-of-hand tricks helped patients improve their dexterity, coordination, and thinking skills. Above all it made therapy sessions, which often can be a painful grind, fun. Patients found themselves motivated to push beyond their previous limits. Naming the program Project Magic, Copperfield consulted with doctors and therapists to tailor tricks to particular forms of disability. Project Magic is now in use in hundreds of hospitals worldwide. Whenever possible, Copperfield enjoys working with patients himself and sometimes will even share a trade secret. One therapist calls the process "Rehabracadabra."[33]

Copperfield's love of the history of magic also led him to create his own museum dedicated to the art. The International Museum and Library of the Conjuring Arts began in 1991, when Copperfield acquired the Mulholland Library, a collection of fifteen thousand magic-related items, for $2.2 million. The items included props such as Houdini's famous oversize milk can, stage machinery, magic kits, posters, handbills, books, and videos. Copperfield moved the collection into a two-story Las Vegas warehouse and continued to add memorabilia over the years. Today the museum holds more than eighty thousand pieces. For now the collection is reserved only for special visitors. "It's become the largest collection of its kind in the world," says Copperfield. "Whenever anybody serious wants to do research on the history of magic, they come here. We've had Hollywood writers and directors here when they wanted research on Houdini for their movies."[34] Copperfield has established a fund to keep the collection intact and hopes someday it will be housed in the Smithsonian Institution in Washington, DC.

Another large project developed by Copperfield is the Musha Cay resort located on eleven private islands in the Caribbean. There he has designed magical effects to entertain guests, such as a huge silver screen that rises from a sandy beach to display his favorite Hollywood movies. Ever the canny entertainer, Copperfield still knows how to delight an audience.

CHAPTER 5

Ning Cai

Outside a large arena at night in downtown Singapore (the name of both the nation and its capital), a slim young woman sits inside a tall metal cage. Her face is covered with a black hood, her bare arms are shackled and lifted above her head, and her neck, legs, and ankles are also chained to the cage. A large digital clock high above shows ninety seconds—the amount of time she has before a fearsome array of steel spikes will drop to the floor of the cage and impale her. Her partner calls for the countdown to begin. As four thousand spectators hold their breath, the young woman begins to work at freeing herself from the handcuffs. Thirty seconds elapse before she springs the cuffs loose and tears off the hood. She takes another thirty seconds to unlock the steel collar around her neck. Now she is frantically manipulating the leg irons and ankle cuffs. A few shrieks erupt from the crowd as the digital numbers dwindle—5, 4, 3. . . . At the last possible instant, she frees her ankles and leaps backward out of the cage as the spikes descend with a crash. A fountain of sparks shoot into the air; the audience roars its approval and relief. Magic Babe Ning—as the performer is known in the show business world—waves to the crowd and thanks them for their support. The Impalement Cage is a typical performance for Singapore's only professional female magician: thrilling, death defying, flawlessly executed, and with a sly touch of sex appeal.

Magic as a Childhood Hobby

Ning Cai was born on October 16, 1982, in Singapore. She has described her upbringing in a large family as typical for a Singaporean girl. From her grandmother Ning learned the benefits of hard work and discipline in every area of life. At home her parents spoke only English, unlike her grandmother, whose house was filled with the rapid sounds of Teochew, a Chinese dialect. (Most Singaporean households are bilingual, speaking English and one of the country's other official languages, which include Mandarin, Malay, and Tamil.) Ning was a scrawny child, but scrappy. She did not hesitate to wrestle or play soccer with her older cousins to prove her mettle.

When Ning was five, a Chinese-speaking magician performed for her kindergarten class. Ning and her friends laughed at the man's outrageous stunts and comical stage props. Her interest in magic grew when she saw a very different sort of magician on TV: David Copperfield. Even as a little girl, Ning loved his sophisticated air that made his illusions seem all the more mysterious. She was so entranced by Copperfield that she hung his poster on her bedroom wall. Magic soon became her childhood obsession. "So instead of playing with Barbie dolls, I picked up magic books at the local library and learnt easy magic effects that I could follow in the instructional pictures provided," she remembers. "The plush toys and stuffed animals on my bed would be my unblinking audience."[35]

> "So instead of playing with Barbie dolls, I picked up magic books at the local library and learnt easy magic effects that I could follow in the instructional pictures provided."[35]
>
> —Ning Cai

Like many child magicians, Ning made use of household items for her first tricks: Styrofoam cups, rubber bands, and wadded paper balls. She would practice her magic skills for hours, demonstrating a new trick for her parents only when she had honed it to perfection. They also urged her to perform for visiting relatives and friends. "The elders all found me strange," she says, "but in an endearingly geeky sort of way."[36] At a young age Ning was already becoming a seasoned entertainer. She enjoyed having a secret knowledge of magic tricks that were guaranteed to fool others. Abiding by the unwritten Magician's Code, she refused to reveal her secrets to anyone.

One secret about Ning that her fans might not suspect is that this glamorous performing magician is at heart a nerd with a passion for writing and computers. She developed this passion early in her school career. While attending Methodist Girls' School, a strict institution with high academic standards, Ning became

Ning Cai, also known by the stage name Magic Babe Ning, has performed many daring escapes in her shows. The Singapore-born magician's performances are thrilling, death defying, and flawlessly executed.

president of the computer club. She liked nothing better than to sit quietly in a corner and patiently explore computer software. In her teens, Ning attended Ngee Ann Polytechnic, a prep school with an emphasis on technology. While she was there, her father lost his job; as the eldest child, she was forced to work to help support the family. During these lean years Ning scrambled to keep up with her schoolwork while holding down a job as a waitress. She was advancing toward her diploma at Ngee Ann Polytechnic when she became fascinated with screenwriting. At the suggestion of a boyfriend, she also took classes in marketing. Her work at Polytechnic's Film Media School won her a scholarship; years later she was invited to be in the school's inaugural hall of fame. She went on to earn a degree in mass communications from the Royal Melbourne Institute of Technology, an Australian college with a branch in Singapore. Her family expected Ning to achieve success as a writer and producer of TV dramas.

Charity Performance and a New Partner

Ning's school background in communications and marketing would soon help her forge her own distinct image in the media. In 2004 she returned to magic by doing benefit performances for her favorite charity, the Children's Cancer Foundation. She found it fulfilling to make the young patients laugh and forget for a while about their painful chemotherapy treatments. The work fit with her belief that magic is a powerful tool to make others happy. In short order she also began to play private parties and company events. Her status as Singapore's only female magician made her a novelty, but it was her genuine skill that carried her through. She also helped found the Singapore Magic Circle, the first online magic discussion forum in the country. Suddenly magic was opening doors for Ning in every facet of her life.

In 2006 her third-place finish in a national magic competition drew the attention of JC (Jan-Chung) Sum, who ran a magic production company and managed some of the top magic talents in the region. JC learned about her skill and originality from several magicians and set up an audition. Ning nervously performed close-up tricks for JC and his colleagues, finishing by causing a sheet of newspaper to explode into flames. JC hired her on the spot. Ning went on to discuss her views about stage magic, how she had no interest in slogging through the same old tricks set to the same old music. She had something more contemporary in mind, an approach that was brash and sexy, to go along with the nickname she had received from an ex-boyfriend: Magic Babe Ning. JC agreed her ideas had great potential. But first he wanted her to work up some new effects making use of fire. As Ning recalls,

> I'd a very unorthodox set of skills and hobbies—so JC used them to my advantage. I could spin fire pois [weighted balls on a cord] and deftly work with a fire staff, so the next step was learning how to do fire eating. Initially I was afraid of getting injured because local magicians who did fire eating in their shows would flaunt their oral blisters like battle scars, but I quickly realized it was really about having the proper techniques. Breathe out, not in.[37]

> "I'd a very unorthodox set of skills and hobbies—so JC used them to my advantage."[37]
>
> —Ning Cai

Ning worked with JC sixteen hours a day to perfect her new routines and illusions. Ultimately Ning added not just fire effects to her act but spikes, samurai swords, and other weapons. Dressed in black leather tights or corsets, and occasionally sporting bright pink hair, Ning resembled some space-age martial arts heroine with a taste for magic. It was a far cry from the old conjurer pulling a rabbit out of his hat. JC, a skilled magician himself, not only approved but decided to team up with his new discovery.

A Glamorous New Star

Propelled by Ning's skill, beauty, and dynamic performing style, the duo soon became the highest-paid magicians in Southeast Asia. They regularly played for audiences in the thousands. Ning's

Succeeding in the Male-Dominated World of Magic

At the start of her career, Ning Cai sought out female magicians in Singapore who could advise her on how to succeed in the magic profession. The few females she found, however, served only as assistants. Most were working with their husbands or fathers in small-time acts for charity shows or church functions. The role of these women was to look attractive in sequined tights and hand the male magician whatever he needed—and occasionally to be sawed in half or made to disappear. None had Ning's passion for creating fresh magical effects and performing them for an audience. "I was very disappointed," Ning admits, "but that made me realize I had to find my own way to become the magicienne I wanted to be."

Ning quickly shattered the stereotype of what a woman could do in the industry. She faced criticism from old-school male magicians who questioned her expertise or claimed a female should not be the focal point of a magic act. They also rejected her use of martial arts weapons and fire effects. But Ning thought their tradition of working with flowers, scarves, and rings had become boring and predictable. "[My critics are] also the very same folks who insist on only performing the 'classics of magic' and consider street magic trash," she says. "I suppose at the end of the day . . . old perceptions are hard to change, but times are changing and one must roll with it, or risk being left behind."

Quoted in Tim Quinlan, "Magic Babe Ning: The Inside Magic Celebrity Interview," *Inside Magic*, November 29, 2010. www.insidemagic.com.

parents were skeptical at first of her decision to pursue magic instead of a career in business or media, but they could not deny her amazing success. Ning herself never dreamed she would end up performing elaborate tricks and illusions onstage. "Life is funny that way but you just have to listen to your heart and just follow the signs," she says. "After I met JC, I guess I never looked back."[38]

The duo's partnership proved to be a shrewd business decision. Ning calls it a love-hate relationship, since they share a passion for ethics, hard work, and exciting magic effects but differ in their basic approach. JC learned his conjuring skills mostly from old books and other professional magicians, while Ning, like many of magic's younger performers, was inspired by DVDs and David

Copperfield's TV specials. JC is also steady and practical, unlike Ning, who tends to be a dreamer intent on raising the bar for stage magic. This disparity led to many arguments, but the duo always found a workable compromise. Best of all, the contrast in their personalities made for an interesting chemistry onstage.

As their success grew, the media increasingly focused on Ning's exotic good looks and skimpy costumes. Writers noted that she was utterly unlike the traditional submissive female in magic shows in the way she commanded attention onstage. Ning also began to appear on magazine covers and billboards clutching a sword or flaming lance or with a playing card peeking out from the back pocket of her jeans. The persona of Magic Babe Ning became like a separate identity that she would assume with each performance, a tongue-in-cheek superheroine with magical powers. "Lately I've allowed my own quirky humor [to] slip into my character because she certainly has evolved," she said in 2010. "I think it works well because it lends depth and dimension into her."[39] As Ning admitted in her autobiography, "Magic Babe was my greatest illusion."[40]

> "Magic Babe was my greatest illusion."[40]
>
> —Ning Cai

Clever Illusions and Dangerous Escapes

While the Magic Babe image helped with bookings, Ning also realized that some people would assume her success was due mainly to her looks and that she had to work twice as hard to earn the audience's respect for her magic skills. She and JC were constantly striving to top themselves with clever new illusions and dangerous escapes. One early routine was a variation on sawing a person in half, with Ning separating parts of JC into a number of boxes. In a so-called mega-illusion called the Impossible Teleportation, Ning stood on a rooftop and caused JC to vanish from his place on the street below and reappear seconds later beside her. For a promotion before a crowd of sixteen thousand, Ning and JC magically transported an automobile from a nearby showroom to the stage in less than ten seconds. As a lark and a demonstration of their expertise, the duo would sometimes perform illusions with

Ning and her performance partner swing like acrobats beneath flames. Throughout her career, she has spent a lot of time developing new and better illusions and more dangerous escapes.

record speed. At the 2009 Singapore River Festival, Ning and JC pulled off fifteen large-scale illusions in five minutes.

The pair also excelled at mind-reading stunts and predictions. In 2010 they predicted the winning numbers for a nationwide lottery one week before the actual drawing. Their numbers were sealed in a large red envelope, locked in a clear plastic container,

The Ultimate Inversion

In their intense rehearsal sessions, Ning and JC would often egg each other on to push the boundaries of some routine. "I'll say, why don't you do this 35 feet in the air?" says JC. "And she goes 'okay.' Then I said, you know from 50 feet, it's only 15 feet more, so why don't we do that? Maybe we should also set it on fire so it looks great."

That is how the duo came to perform what they called the Ultimate Inversion. Before twelve thousand fans at the 2013 Singapore Night Festival, Ning and JC were lifted on a crane 75 feet (22.9 m) into the air. Each was hanging upside down in gravity boots (boots secured to a bar) and restrained inside two heavy straitjackets. JC, hanging above Ning, began to get queasy from the height. Meanwhile Ning, although sweating profusely on the warm night, was overcome by a tranquil feeling. She called up to JC to shut his eyes and continued to wriggle free from her straitjackets. She loosened the last strap just as JC's second straitjacket rustled past her head. Everything seemed fine until a sudden jerk downward made her blood run cold. One of the supporting chains had snapped. Ning and JC fought to control their wild swinging motions while the crane rapidly lowered them. Once they were safe on the ground, exhausted and trembling, Ning began to consider a new career.

Quoted in Deborah Choo, "Tech Geek Turns into Singapore's Sexiest Magician," *Yahoo! News*, September 20, 2012. www.yahoo.com.

and hung high above the entrance to a popular Singapore nightclub. Security guards were hired to watch the container around the clock. After the announcement of the winning numbers, the container was lowered and opened to reveal that Ning and JC's prediction matched the numbers exactly. Also inside was a check for $10,000 made out to the Children's Cancer Foundation.

Ning is best known, however, for her daring escapes. She loved to pay tribute to one of her heroes of magic, Houdini, by performing variations of his famous routines. This area of magic also enabled her to use her physical skills and yoga discipline to great effect. In the Water Vault, a pink-haired Ning was locked and chained into a stainless steel cube filled with water. She emerged after three minutes, drenched and with her chest heaving, to wild applause. The Extreme Inversion saw her escape from two straitjackets while hanging upside down from a burning rope 35 feet (10.7 m) above the ground. In the Impalement

Cage, Ning narrowly escaped from a steel cage and a platform of steel spikes timed to fall on her after ninety seconds. This mega-escape, first performed in July 2008, helped launch the duo's Ultimate Magic show, which had a long run in Singapore's largest entertainment district.

A New Direction

To the shock and disappointment of her fans, Ning retired from performing magic in 2014. "Time flies and it has been a great 10-year run for me," she wrote on her Facebook page. "Looking back, I'm really happy and content with all the awards and achievements I've made as a successful woman in this traditionally male-dominated industry."[41] She had certainly enjoyed a remarkable career, performing and giving lectures on magic throughout Europe, Asia, and the Middle East. Ning also had won numerous awards, including the 2012 Singapore Women's Weekly Great Women of Our Time award. She got married one month after announcing her retirement, and the next year she published her autobiography, *Who Is Magic Babe Ning?* In 2016 she was nominated for the Singapore Literature Prize. The glamorous extrovert was more than ready to give way to her bookish, nerdy self and concentrate on writing. Today Ning is excited about her new life. "There were nights when looking into the mirror as I was wiping off my stage makeup, I didn't know who I was anymore or why I wanted things the old me wouldn't," she says. "But the most important thing in life is contentment."[42] Her final trick, alas, was to make Magic Babe Ning disappear.

> "There were nights when looking into the mirror as I was wiping off my stage makeup, I didn't know who I was anymore or why I wanted things the old me wouldn't."[42]
>
> —*Ning Cai*

CHAPTER 6

Criss Angel

The magician wears faded baggy jeans, a black vest, and a huge silver chain around his neck. With a few lulling phrases he causes a crowd of perhaps two hundred inside a glass-roofed pavilion to go into a hypnotic trance, asleep and frozen in place. Then, as a camera crew follows him, he begins to weave his illusion. First, he causes a girl in black to bend backward at the waist and remain floating in an almost impossible position. He moves on to make a man rise a few inches above the stool he was sitting on. He levitates a woman until she is suspended in air parallel to the ground. At a touch from the magician, another girl seems to go weightless and floats several feet above the pavilion floor. He finally gestures toward a third girl on a stairway, causing her to rise 20 feet (6.1 m) in the air and remain there motionless and apparently asleep. A woman who has arrived after the hypnotic spell is witnessing what is going on and is virtually speechless with astonishment. A national TV audience shares her sense of wonder. Criss Angel, one of the greatest illusionists of his generation, has pulled off another of what he calls a *mindfreak*—a mystifying effect performed in ordinary surroundings. It is magic freed from the stage and moved out among the people to create an uncanny new type of reality show.

Magic as Secret Knowledge

Christopher Nicholas Sarantakos, the future Criss Angel, was born on December 19, 1967, in East Meadow, New York, on Long Island. Christopher's Greek American family included his parents, John and Dimitra, and his two brothers, Costa and J.D. From his father, Christopher learned at an early age the value of hard work. John Sarantakos owned a restaurant and donut shop and also found time for daily workouts. From his aunt Stella, Christopher learned about magic; he was seven when she taught him his first card trick. He loved the sense of magic as secret knowledge. "From that day on, I was hooked," he says. "I felt this incredible sense of power that an adult didn't understand how it worked, but I did."[43] Hours of practice and study led to his first show five years later at a neighborhood birthday party. The young magician earned ten dollars.

It was a small fee, but it made him a professional magician, like his idol, Harry Houdini. Soon he began taking the train to Manhattan to explore magic shops and seek out auditions. By age fourteen he was playing weekly shows at bars and restaurants around Long Island, often making as much as a hundred dollars a night in tips. Christopher's parents delighted in their son's hobby, particularly when he performed a household illusion, such as making his mother float above her chair. However, when Christopher announced his plans to skip college after graduating from East Meadow High, his parents were not pleased. "The thought of my becoming a professional magician was unbearable for them," he admits. "They had hoped their three sons would go to college and become doctors or lawyers—but not a magician!"[44] Despite their misgivings, Christopher hit the road and joined the circuit of performing acts. He combined practical learning on the stage with hours of study at local libraries, poring over books about classic magicians and their trademark effects. He hoped someday to be included among their special company. With this in mind he began calling himself

> "I felt this incredible sense of power that an adult didn't understand how [magic tricks] worked, but I did."[43]
>
> —Criss Angel

Criss Angel—a name he found more suitable for billboards and marquees.

Breakthrough on TV

In 1994, after years of small-time bookings, Angel got his first major break in show business. He presented his magic skills on *Secrets*, a prime-time network TV special that explained some of the tricks employed by professional illusionists. Angel's performance came to the attention of Clive Barker, a writer and director on themes of horror. Barker hired Angel as a consultant on his next film, *Lord of Illusions*. The two also worked together on Angel's first musical album. By this time Angel had adopted the look of a rock star, sporting an all-black wardrobe, long hair, heavy eye makeup, and ornate medallions. His obsessive workouts in the gym—a legacy from his father—helped him maintain an athlete's physique.

Angel's stamina came in handy in 1998, when he headlined New York City's annual Halloween convention at Madison Square Garden. For the entire twelve days of the convention, he performed his ten-minute show *Criss Angel: World of Illusion* sixty times a day with dogged precision. "I was exhausted at the end of the run," he says. "This was definitely one of those things that I had no idea what I was signing up for when I agreed to do 60 shows a day."[45] Nonetheless, the engagement led to an even more prestigious booking in New York. In 2001 he began a three-year run with *Criss Angel: Mindfreak* at the World Underground Theater in Times Square. He was able to showcase the range of his magic talents, from close-up effects to larger illusions. He caused members of the audience to float in the air, produced doves from his empty hands, changed the denominations of paper money, and vanished and reappeared at will. The word *mindfreak* expressed his edgy, psychological approach to the

"I felt like I wanted to coin a term that would be basically the reaction to my art. It would be a mindfreak and so that's why I came up with that."[46]

—*Criss Angel*

The illusionist Criss Angel specializes in mystifying effects performed in ordinary surroundings. He calls these types of tricks mindfreaks.

art of magic. "I came up with the term 'mindfreak' because I didn't like the word 'magician,'" he told an interviewer. "I felt like I wanted to coin a term that would be basically the reaction to my art. It would be a mindfreak and so that's why I came up with that. But, many people say I'm really a student of humanity and psychology."[46]

Street Magic and Baffling Illusions

Soon after Angel's New York show closed, TV came calling again. In 2005 he adapted *Criss Angel: Mindfreak* into a reality TV series for the cable network A&E. For the show Angel moved to Las Vegas, where he often took to the streets with a handheld camera to perform his sleight-of-hand magic and illusions for unwitting pedestrians. The street setting gave his effects a tossed-off, nonchalant air that made them seem all the more baffling. Video clips from the show became favorites on YouTube and other Internet sites. The series ran for five seasons and made Angel a star. For many viewers the punkish black-clad magician with the wedge of dark hair over one eye had established himself as the new face of professional magic. And he was not above offering his fans a glimpse at how certain tricks were done. As TV critic Steve West noted, "Criss' candor with his fans about what he does is a big part of the appeal. It's inspiring to fans of the art form to see someone with passion share his innermost trickery, and [he] still leaves you in awe."[47]

Mindfreak helped spur new interest in magic, becoming part of a larger trend in TV, movies, and books. For the series Angel produced some of his best-known escapes and illusions. To promote the show's third season, he traveled to Times Square in New York City for a special escape. Angel, in handcuffs, first wriggled into a steel case that was four feet in diameter and the case was lifted by crane four stories into the air. The box then was filled with concrete—6,000 pounds' (2,722 kg) worth. It was timed to drop to the street below exactly twenty-four hours after Angel had closed himself inside. As the deadline approached, a large crowd gathered to count down the final seconds. Shrieks erupted as time ran out and the concrete-filled case crashed to the ground. When nothing happened for several seconds, the people grew silent, suspecting something had gone wrong. Then Angel appeared, waving to his fans from a scaffolding some distance away from the fallen box. The relieved crowd roared its approval.

Angel loves to carry out his illusions in unusual settings. For instance, he changed takeout cups of coffee into cockroaches

Confronting His Fears

In the course of his career Criss Angel has performed dozens of risky escapes and illusions. He has been encased in concrete, locked in a water cell, hung by his ankles in twin straitjackets, and chained to the balcony of a hotel about to be demolished. Angel seems to be the model of the fearless magician. But he admits to having worked hard to conquer his fears. In this he says his greatest inspiration has been his father, John, who was diagnosed with stomach cancer and given three weeks to live. Instead John lived three more years, enjoying life as much as he possibly could. "He really was a firm believer that the mind controlled the body, that the body was a slave if you will to the mind," Angel says. "Each and every moment of his life he had a smile on his face. . . . He was in tremendous pain, couldn't even swallow, and yet just had a positive attitude."

After his father died in his arms, Angel set about to face his own worst fears. One of these was a fear of needles. He would pass out from getting blood drawn. He confronted this fear as only Criss Angel could—by hanging suspended in Times Square from eight fishhooks. For his TV show *Mindfreak*, he hung from a helicopter held only by four fishhooks embedded in his bare back. Angel hopes that his example will help others face their own fears and overcome them.

Quoted in Steve West, "Interview with the Mindfreak Criss Angel," *CinemaBlend*. www.cinemablend.com.

outside a New York City diner. He split a woman in two before a gathering in a public park. He casually walked across the surface of a swimming pool at a Las Vegas hotel. He hung from a helicopter, supported only by four fish hooks sunk into his bare back, more than 1,000 feet (305 m) above the Valley of Fire in southeast Nevada. And, in one of his favorite illusions, he levitated himself more than 500 feet (152 m) into the air above Las Vegas Boulevard, bathed in the blinding pillar of light over the Luxor Hotel.

Angel admits that his stunts for the camera in front of live audiences can be especially difficult. "I think, you know, performing on the streets, whether it's on the sidewalk in Las Vegas, in the parking lot, or on a mountain, what have you, it certainly has its challenges because I have sometimes thousands of people watching a particular demonstration," he says. "Each of them pretty much has a cell phone, a camera. When we're around

Wearing handcuffs, Angel prepares for a death-defying escape from a concrete-filled steel case hoisted four stories above New York City's Times Square. When, as part of the act, the case was allowed to crash to the ground, Angel miraculously appeared before the crowd some distance away.

buildings, you have people shooting from all different aspects and angles. I have to really be on top of my game, because we live in a technological age."[48]

Mixed Reviews with Cirque du Soleil

Angel's next project saw him at less than the top of his game— at least according to many critics. In 2006, with *Mindfreak* still going strong, he joined with Cirque du Soleil, a Canadian performance group, to create a new live show at the Luxor Hotel in Las

Vegas. *Criss Angel Believe* featured Angel's magical effects and Cirque du Soleil's high-wire acrobatics. The name of the show referred to Angel's hero, Harry Houdini, who told his wife if he could contact her from the afterlife he would use the code word "believe." Reviews of the show were mixed, with many critics noting it had a confusing theme and that Angel's illusions were sparse and lacked their usual verve. When one gossip writer in attendance tweeted that *Believe* was unbelievably bad, Angel began hurling insults at him from the stage. Despite the poor notices, *Believe* proved to be a long-running success, earning $150 million in 2010 alone.

In 2007 Angel got the opportunity to channel Houdini in another way on the reality series *Phenomenon*. Angel served as a judge while contestants tried to prove their psychic abilities on live TV. Like Houdini, Angel loves to expose frauds and cranks. When one contestant claimed to have genuine psychic powers, Angel challenged him to a test. He offered the man $1 million if he could name the message on a card in a sealed envelope. The man failed, and Angel opened the envelope to reveal he had written "9-11." Angel made the point that if psychic powers really existed—which he refuses to believe—disasters like the terrorist attacks on September 11, 2001, might have been averted.

A Last Major Escape

Angel's last major escape act might have impressed Houdini himself. In 2008 he handcuffed himself to a sixth-floor balcony railing on the abandoned Spyglass Resort hotel on Clearwater Beach, Florida. Four minutes after he locked the cuffs, dynamite charges laid throughout the old hotel were set to go off and implode the building. Angel was supposed to free himself from the cuffs, race up three floors to the rooftop, and escape by helicopter seconds before the demolition. However, as fifty thousand people looked on, the helicopter flew off without Angel just as the implosions collapsed the building. Film crews scoured the rubble for several tense minutes. Finally Angel, covered in dust and walking gingerly, emerged from the wreckage. He explained to the TV audience that he had failed to pick the padlock on the rooftop door in time to be picked up by the helicopter. It was left to the people's imagination whether he had actually endured the implosion. According to the *Tampa Bay Times*, "Angel repeated Wednesday night that the Harry Houdini-style stunt would be his last dangerous one, in deference to his mother. He said he didn't want her to worry anymore."[49]

Angel could not avoid risky routines, however. In 2014 he suffered a severe shoulder injury during a broadcast from Times Square in which he was hanging upside down and trying to escape from two straitjackets weighted with iron. He had to undergo surgery to repair a torn right rotator cuff and a torn left bicep. His fans, who call themselves the Loyals, flooded the Internet with prayers and good wishes for their idol. Like magicians throughout history, Angel vowed to regale them with even more

The Secret of Levitating

Criss Angel's most spectacular levitating feats employ ultrathin wires and a crane off camera that lifts him high into the air. His more modest floating illusions actually use more clever means. First of all, Angel plants a strong magnet inside the heel of each shoe. The shoes must stick together when Angel puts his feet together. Next, Angel cuts a slit, from the top of the thigh to the ankle, in the front of one leg of his black pants. The slit must be unobtrusive—opening just enough for his foot to slip through. Angel wears black tights underneath that blend with the pants.

Angel then stands in front of a chair or small platform with his back to the audience. He brings his feet together so that the magnets hold the shoes together. He mimes great effort and sometimes raises his arms in the air to direct the audience's attention away from his shoes. Then he will slip his foot onto the platform and lift the other foot into the air behind him. From behind, the audience sees both his shoes rise in the air, and it looks as if Angel is floating several inches off the ground. He can even hover in place for a few seconds. To land, Angel brings both shoes, still magnetized together, down onto the platform. The landing is on slightly bent knees, to simulate great effort. As the audience applauds, Angel slips his foot back into the empty shoe and pulls his feet apart.

fantastic illusions in the future. "When a demonstration can transport us beyond questions of how it is done, then it becomes the purest form of magic—the magic of emotion," he says. "Most of all, magic is in our cultural DNA."[50]

Although performing magic remains his obsession, Angel put his career on hold in October 2015 to be with his two-year-old son, Johnny Crisstopher Sarantakos, at a cancer center near Angel's home in Australia. Johnny was diagnosed with acute lymphoblastic leukemia, a type of cancer that most commonly affects children. Doctors announced that Johnny's cancer went into remission in the spring of 2016. Angel fervently hopes that his son will have a full recovery—a real-life escape to outdo any of Angel's theatrical effects.

> "When a demonstration can transport us beyond questions of how it is done, then it becomes the purest form of magic—the magic of emotion."[50]
>
> —Criss Angel

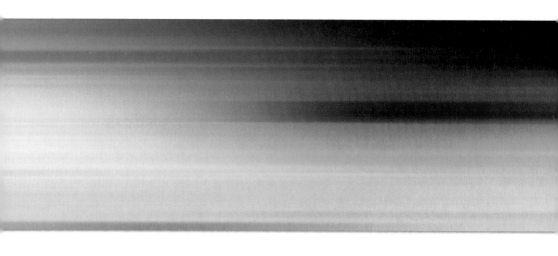

SOURCE NOTES

Introduction: The Pleasure of Being Fooled

1. Quoted in Antony Funnell, "The Magic of Technology, the Technology of Magic," *Future Tense*, April 15, 2014. www.abc.net.au.
2. Alex Stone, *Fooling Houdini: Magicians, Mentalists, Math Geeks & the Hidden Powers of the Mind*. New York: HarperCollins, 2012, p. 6.
3. Jim Steinmeyer, *Hiding the Elephant: How Magicians Invented the Impossible and Learned to Disappear*. New York: Carroll & Graf, 2003, p. 17.

Chapter 1: Harry Houdini

4. Quoted in *Encyclopedia of World Biography*, "Harry Houdini Biography." www.notablebiographies.com.
5. Quoted in William Kalush and Larry Sloman, *The Secret Life of Houdini: The Making of America's First Superhero*. New York: Atria, 2006, p. 39.
6. Quoted in Warren Manger, "When a Man from the Mirror Trapped Harry Houdini—but Not for Long," *Mirror* (London), October 5, 2013. www.mirror.co.uk.
7. Quoted in Manger, "When a Man from the Mirror Trapped Harry Houdini—but Not for Long."
8. Sid Fleischman, *The Story of the Great Houdini*. New York: Harper-Collins, 2006, p. 6.

9. Allison Meier, "Houdini's Milk Can Escape, Where Failure Meant Death by Drowning," *Atlas Obscura*, April 19, 2013. www.atlasob scura.com.

10. Quoted in Kalush and Sloman, *The Secret Life of Houdini*, p. 212.

Chapter 2: Penn & Teller

11. YouTube, "Penn & Teller—Helium Escape," May 13, 2013. www .youtube.com/watch?v=ZNrhGgrGi0c.

12. Quoted in Benjamin Secher, "Penn and Teller Interview," *Telegraph* (London), July 9, 2010. www.telegraph.co.uk.

13. Quoted in Lee Cowan, "Why Penn & Teller Need Each Other," CBS News, January 25, 2015. www.cbsnews.com.

14. Quoted in Nick A. Zaino III, "Penn & Teller's Popularity Is No Illusion," *Boston Globe*, January 23, 2014. www.bostonglobe.com.

15. Quoted in Zaino III, "Penn & Teller's Popularity Is No Illusion."

16. Quoted in Zaino III, "Penn & Teller's Popularity Is No Illusion."

17. Quoted in Marco R. Della Cava, "At Home: Teller's Magical Vegas Retreat Speaks Volumes," *USA Today*, November 16, 2007. http://usatoday30.usatoday.com.

18. Quoted in Secher, "Penn and Teller Interview."

19. Quoted in Cowan, "Why Penn & Teller Need Each Other."

Chapter 3: Ricky Jay

20. Quoted in Mark Singer, "Secrets of the Magus," *New Yorker*, April 5, 1993. www.newyorker.com.

21. Quoted in Stephen Whitty, "Ricky Jay: Behind the Mysteries of a Master Magician," NJ.com, April 14, 2013. www.nj.com.

22. Quoted in Whitty, "Ricky Jay."

23. Quoted in Singer, "Secrets of the Magus."

24. Quoted in Singer, "Secrets of the Magus."

25. Quoted in Singer, "Secrets of the Magus."

26. Quoted in Whitty, "Ricky Jay."

27. Quoted in PBS, *Ricky Jay: Deceptive Practice, PBS—American Masters*, film, January 23, 2015.

Chapter 4: David Copperfield

28. Quoted in Stan Allen, "David Copperfield Discusses Hospitalization, Brush with Death and More," *Las Vegas (NV) Sun*, September 28, 2012. http://lasvegassun.com.

29. Quoted in Allen, "David Copperfield Discusses Hospitalization, Brush with Death and More."
30. J. Walker, "Same as It Ever Was?: How the 21st Century Made David Copperfield Disappear," *This Was Television*, May 29, 2013. http://thiswastv.com.
31. Walker, "Same as It Ever Was?"
32. Quoted in DavidCopperfield.com, "David Copperfield Biography." www.davidcopperfield.com.
33. Creative Therapies, "Rehabracadabra: Using Magic and Other Creative Therapies to Maximize Functional Outcomes." www.creative therapies.com.
34. Quoted in Robin Leach, "Inside David Copperfield's Holy Grail of Wizardry in Las Vegas," *Las Vegas (NV) Sun*, June 4, 2011. http://lasvegassun.com.

Chapter 5: Ning Cai

35. Quoted in Tim Quinlan, "Magic Babe Ning: The Inside Magic Celebrity Interview," *Inside Magic*, November 29, 2010. www.inside magic.com.
36. Quoted in Quinlan, "Magic Babe Ning: The Inside Magic Celebrity Interview."
37. Quoted in Quinlan, "Magic Babe Ning: The Inside Magic Celebrity Interview."
38. Quoted in Deborah Choo, "Tech Geek Turns into Singapore's Sexiest Magician," *Yahoo! News*, September 20, 2012. www.yahoo.com.
39. Quoted in Quinlan, "Magic Babe Ning: The Inside Magic Celebrity Interview."
40. Quoted in Belinda Ho, "Review: Who Is Magic Babe Ning? by Ning Cai," NingThing.com, http://ningthing.com.
41. Quoted in Christopher Toh, "Magic Babe Ning: No More Magic," *Today*, November 7, 2014. www.todayonline.com.
42. Quoted in Toh, "Magic Babe Ning: No More Magic."

Chapter 6: Criss Angel

43. Quoted in *bio*, "Criss Angel Biography," *bio*. www.biography.com.
44. Quoted in *Las Vegas Sun*, "Criss Angel Biography," *Las Vegas Sun*. http://lasvegassun.com.

45. Quoted in *Las Vegas Sun*, "Criss Angel Biography."
46. Quoted in Jeanne Wolf, "Interview with Criss Angel," *Parade*, August 28, 2007. http://parade.com.
47. Quoted in Steve West, "Criss Angel's Mindfreak Prepares for Third Season," *CinemaBlend*, www.cinemablend.com.
48. Quoted in Rebecca Harper, "Exclusive Interview with Criss Angel: Mindfreak," *Hulu Blog*, August 26, 2009. http://blog.hulu.com.
49. Mike Donila and Jackie Alexander, "Criss Angel Escapes an Imploding Hotel—but Not as Expected," *Tampa Bay Times*, July 30, 2008. www.tampabay.com.
50. Criss Angel, "The Unbroken Spell of Magic," *Huffington Post*, May 21, 2013. www.huffingtonpost.com.

FOR FURTHER RESEARCH

Books

Criss Angel, *Mindfreak: Secret Revelations*. New York: HarperCollins, 2008.

Ning Cai, *Who Is Magic Babe Ning?* New York: Cavendish Editions, 2015.

William Kalush and Larry Sloman, *The Secret Life of Houdini: The Making of America's First Superhero*. New York: Atria, 2007.

Jim Steinmeyer, *Hiding the Elephant: How Magicians Invented the Impossible and Learned to Disappear*. New York: Carroll & Graf, 2004.

Alex Stone, *Fooling Houdini: Magicians, Mentalists, Math Geeks & the Hidden Powers of the Mind*. New York: HarperCollins, 2012.

Internet Sources

Lee Cowan, "Why Penn & Teller Need Each Other," CBS News, January 25, 2015. www.cbsnews.com/news/why-penn-teller-need-each-other.

Jefferson Graham, "Copperfield Conjures New Tricks from Tech," *USA Today*, January 20, 2015. www.usatoday.com/story/tech/columnist/talkingtech/2015/01/19/david-copperfield-conjures-tricks-from-tech/21865713.

Devon Maloney, "Ask a Magician: How Hard Is It to Make It in the Illusion Game These Days?," *Vulture*, March 15, 2013. www.vulture.com/2013/03/how-hard-is-it-to-make-it-as-a-magician-today.html.

Jennifer McKee, "How Criss Angel Became the Most Watched Magician in Television History," *Where Traveler*, September 17, 2014. www.wheretraveler.com/las-vegas/how-criss-angel-became-most-watched-magician-television-history.

Allison Meier, "Houdini's Milk Can Escape, Where Failure Meant Death by Drowning," *Atlas Obscura*, April 19, 2013. www.atlasobscura.com/articles/houdini-milk-can-at-the-american-museum-of-magic.

Websites

All About Magicians (www.all-about-magicians.com). This website focuses on biographies of magicians and illusionists. It includes a magic time line and separate categories for female magicians, street magicians, cardicians (magicians who work with playing cards), escape artists, and mega-illusionists.

Magic Secrets Explained (www.secrets-explained.com). This site is filled with videos that explain many of the basic tricks and illusions used by professional magicians. It presents basic techniques that every magician learns, and includes sections on card tricks, coin tricks, and rope tricks. The site also examines the effects of famous illusionists such as Criss Angel, David Blaine, David Copperfield, and Penn & Teller.

Magicpedia (http://geniimagazine.com). This online encyclopedia of magic is made for the browsing enthusiast. It includes biographies of more than thirty-four hundred performers, listings of more than seventeen hundred books on magic, and a fascinating section that categorizes illusions alphabetically, with titles like "Appearing Elephant," "Clearly Impossible," and "Miser's Dream."

World Wide Website of Ricky Jay (www.rickyjay.com). This is a wide-ranging collection of material curated by the great sleight-of-hand magician Ricky Jay. It includes Jay's biography, news about his upcoming films and appearances, museum exhibits based on his collection of magic-related items, and many other entertaining odds and ends.

INDEX

PICTURE CREDITS

ABOUT THE AUTHOR

John Allen is a writer living in Oklahoma City.